Treasury of Ironwork Designs

469 Examples from Historical Sources

Selected and Arranged by
Carol Belanger Grafton

DOVER PUBLICATIONS, INC.
New York

Published in Canada by General Publishing Company, Ltd., 30 Lesmill Road, Don Mills, Toronto, Ontario.

Treasury of Ironwork Designs: 469 Examples from Historical Sources is a new work, first published by Dover Publications, Inc., in 1992.

DOVER *Pictorial Archive* SERIES

Manufactured in the United States of America
Dover Publications, Inc., 31 East 2nd Street, Mineola, N.Y. 11501

Library of Congress Cataloging-in-Publication Data

Grafton, Carol Belanger.
    Treasury of ironwork designs : 469 examples from historical sources / selected and arranged by Carol Belanger Grafton.
        p.   cm. — (Dover pictorial archive series)
    ISBN 0-486-27126-9 (pbk.)
    1. Architectural ironwork.   I. Title.   II. Series.
NA3950.G74   1992
739.4′8—dc20   92-10134
                                                                              CIP

PUBLISHER'S NOTE

THE STRENGTH, PERMANENCE AND BEAUTY of iron have ensured its incorporation into Western architecture through many centuries. Structural and "fixtural" ironwork, both decorative and functional, reached its peak in the nineteenth century, when the Industrial Revolution led to its use on a scale hitherto unknown. Though genuine wrought iron has always remained a handcraft, cast iron, produced with molds, lent itself easily to true mass production.

The taste of the era embraced, in every medium, the most historically diverse styles. These were illustrated in the countless books, catalogues and journals of the "decorative arts"—all providing numerous designs for reproduction or purchase—that accompanied this burgeoning industrial output. The present volume thus includes examples stemming from the Middle Ages mingled with products of the Art Nouveau sensibility and specimens of every era in between. The principal sources of the images were the fifth *Catalogue of MacFarlane's Castings*, published by Walter MacFarlane & Co. of Glasgow, and the French decorative-arts journal *L'Art Pour Tous*. A handful of designs were taken from other publications—*Harper's Monthly*, *Art Journal*, the *Illustrated London News* and the catalogue of the Seville firm of Antonio Aguilar, among others.

The fixtures and structural elements depicted are diverse: balustrades, banisters, fences and railings; doors and gates; balconies; crestings and finials; window grilles, transoms and fanlights; spandrels and brackets; panels; stairs; marquees; signs; lamps; columns; and roof hip and curb plates.

The unusual beauty of Paris, New Orleans, Seville, Brussels and other cities owes much to their superb and ubiquitous ironwork. And if today ironwork has largely ceased to figure in new architectural design, this in no way reflects on its inherent utility and economy; none of the materials that have supplanted it has approached its combination of qualities. The exquisite tracery strong enough to defy the elements and the vandals may yet reclaim its former place in the urban landscape.

I

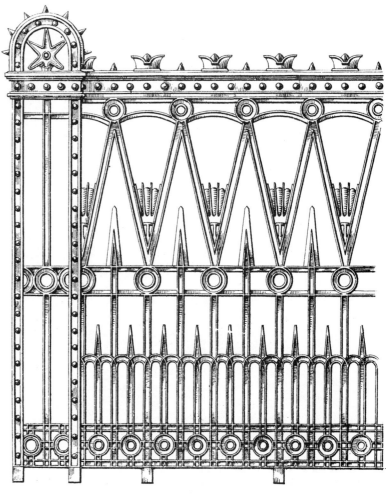

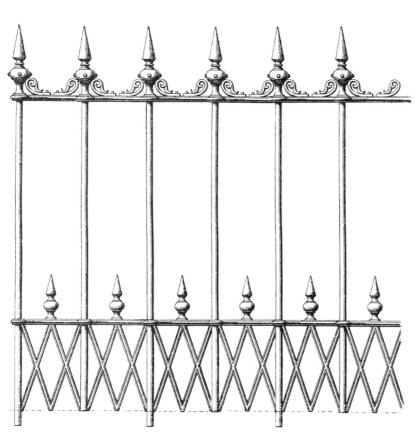

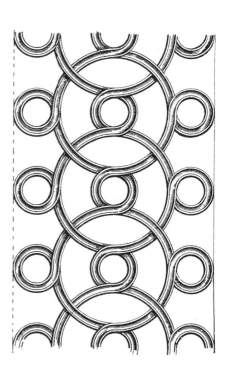

11

12

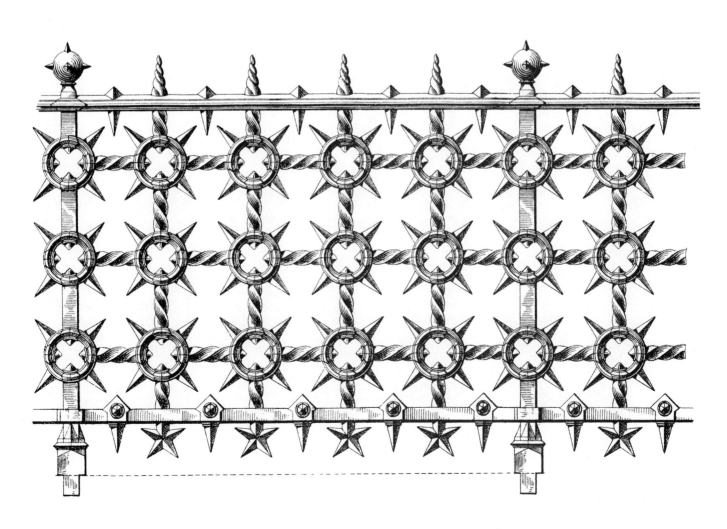

13

15

16

H. La Nave

Ruckert Sc.

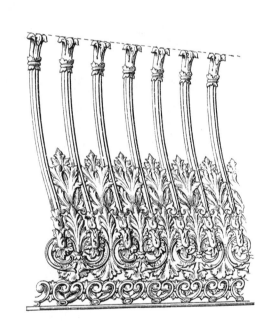

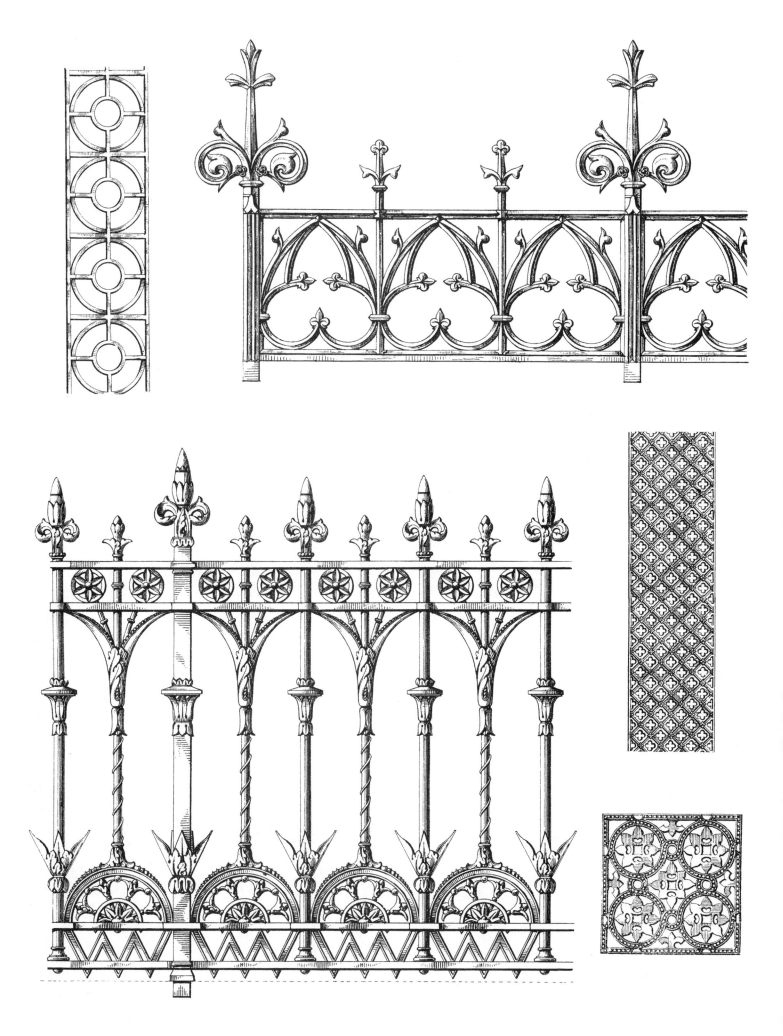

22

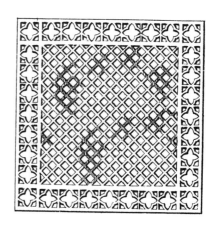

24

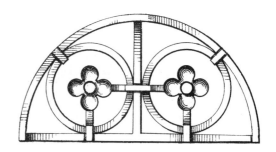
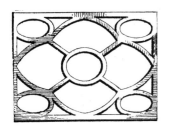

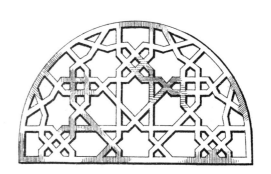

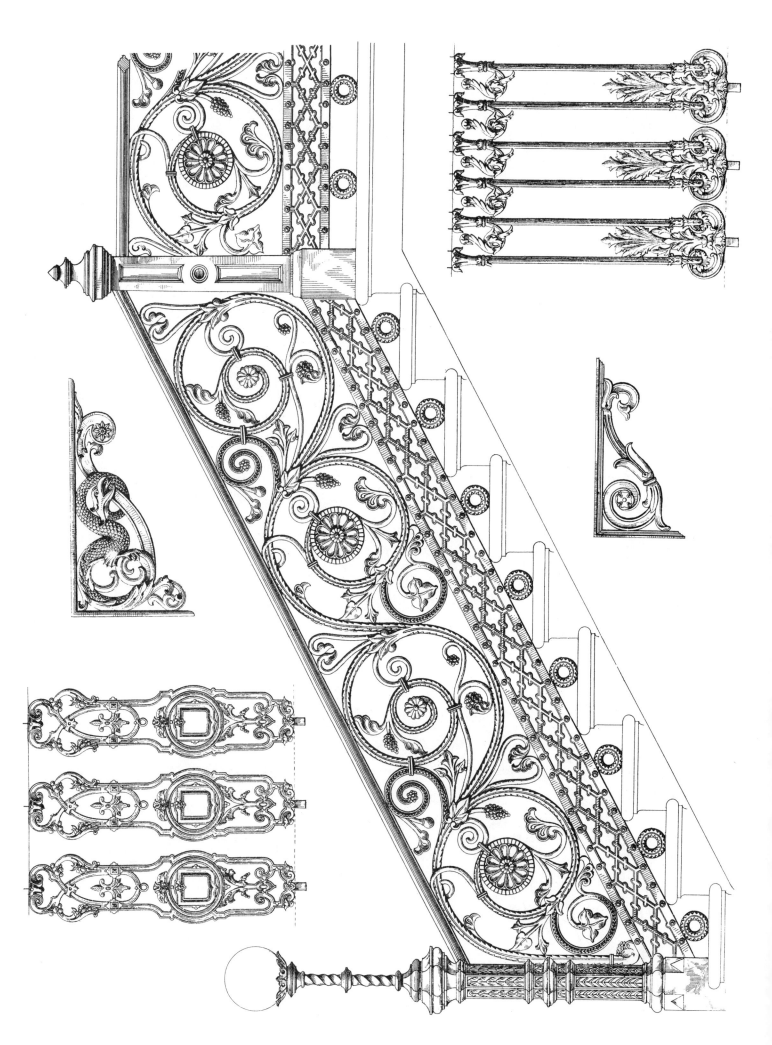

26

27

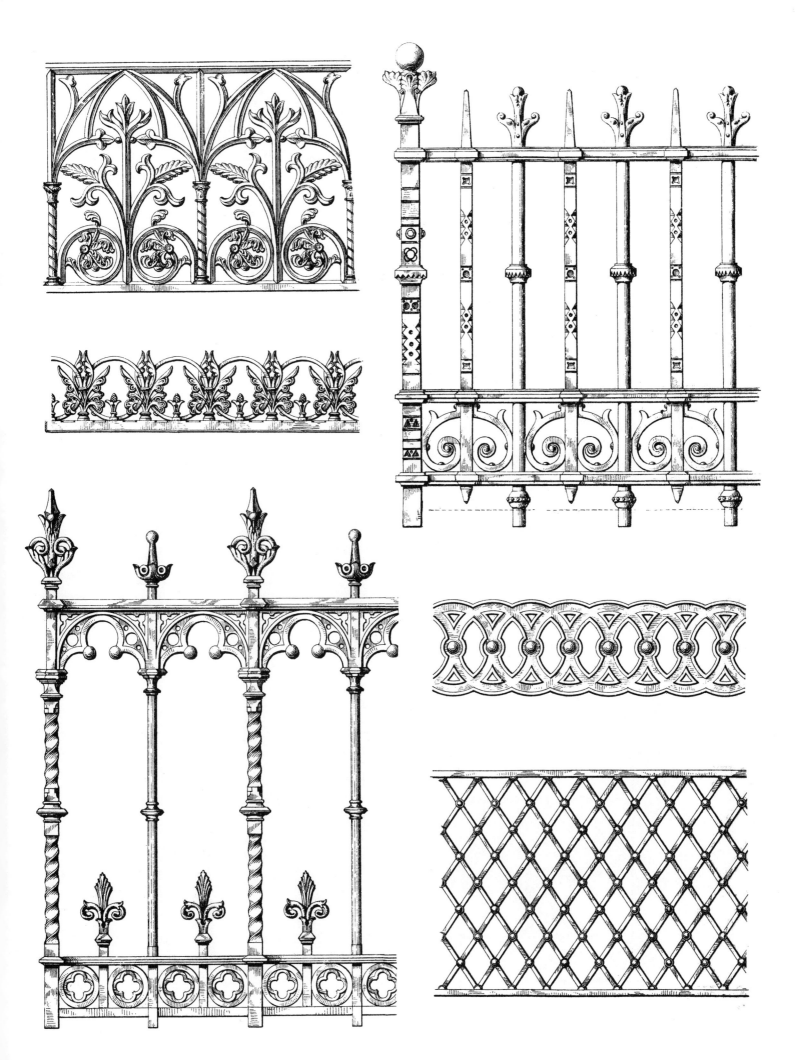

29

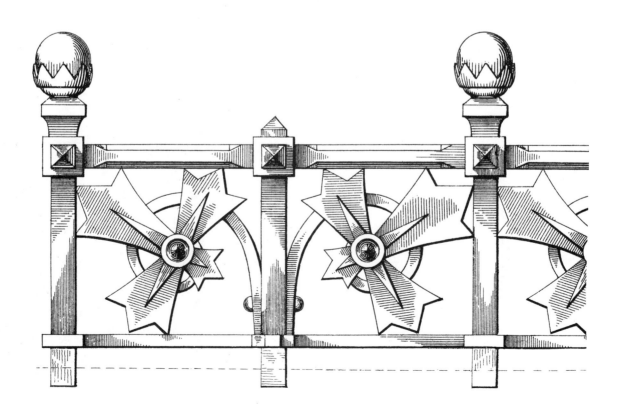

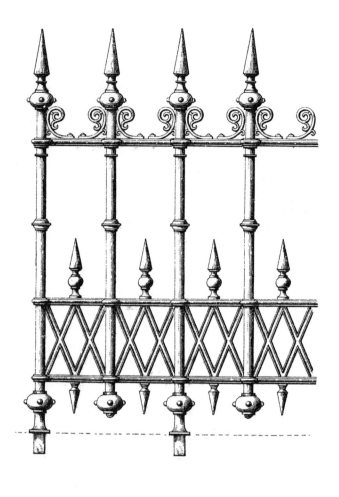

33

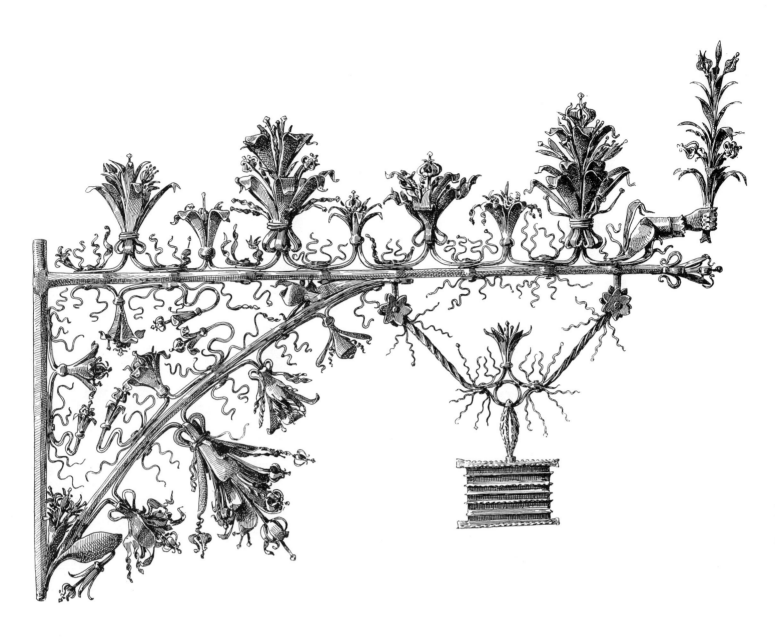

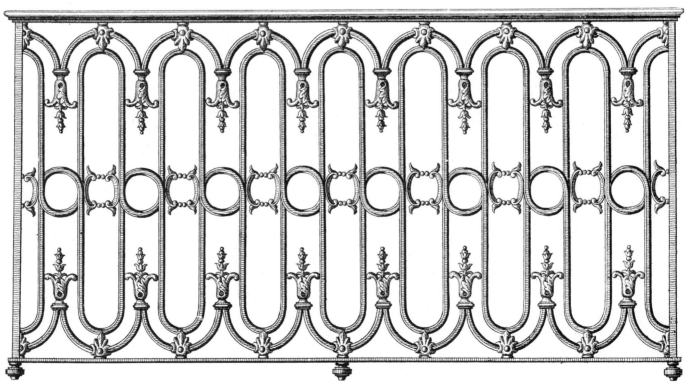

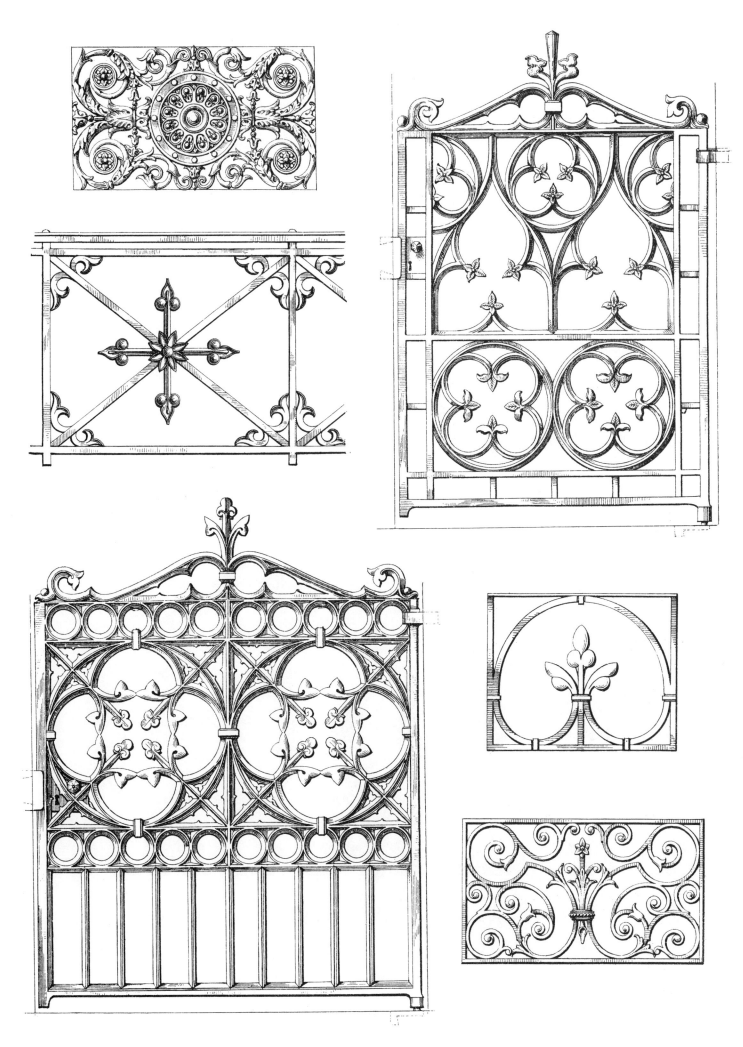

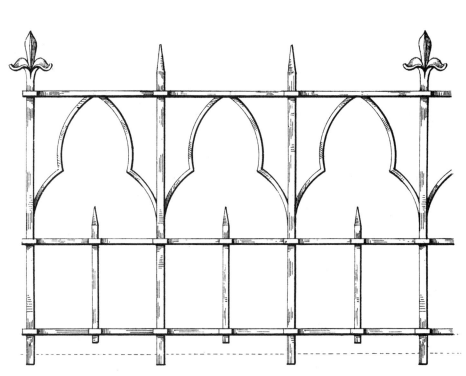

39

41

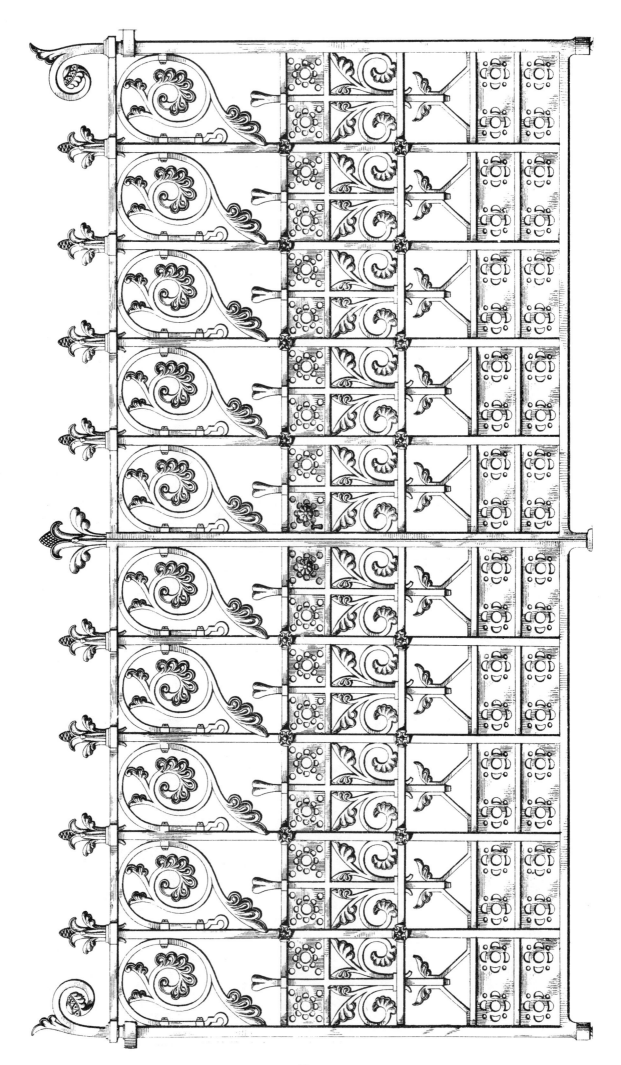

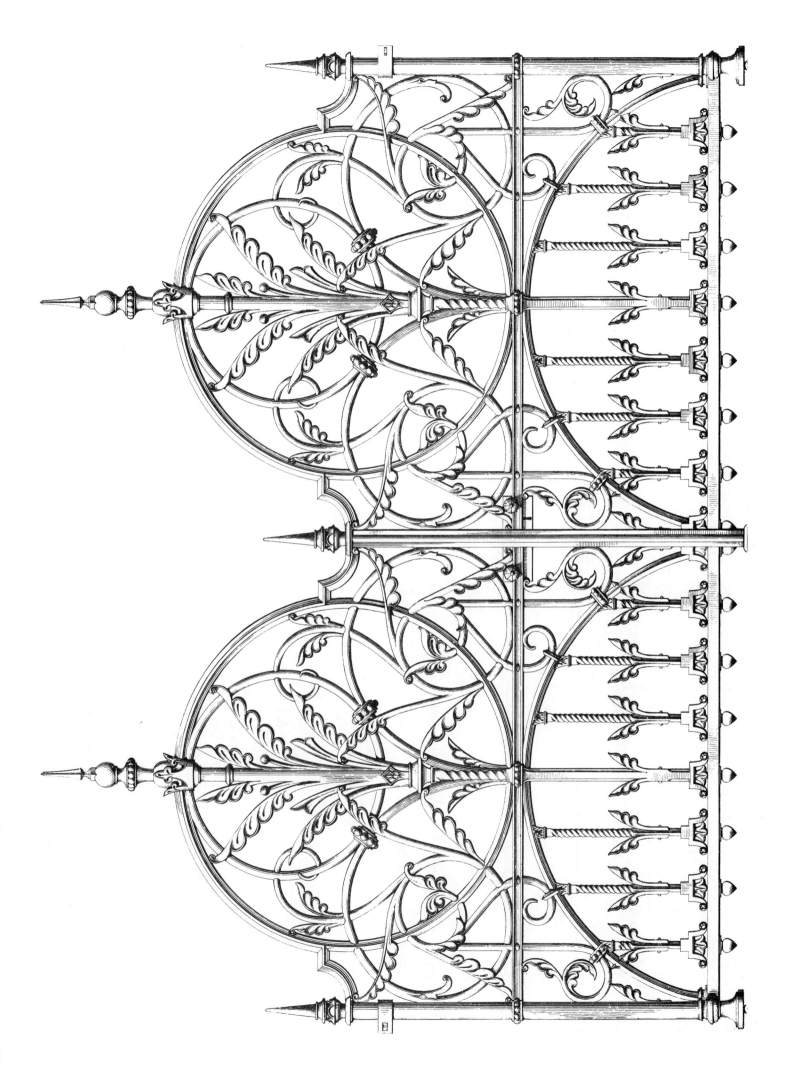

43

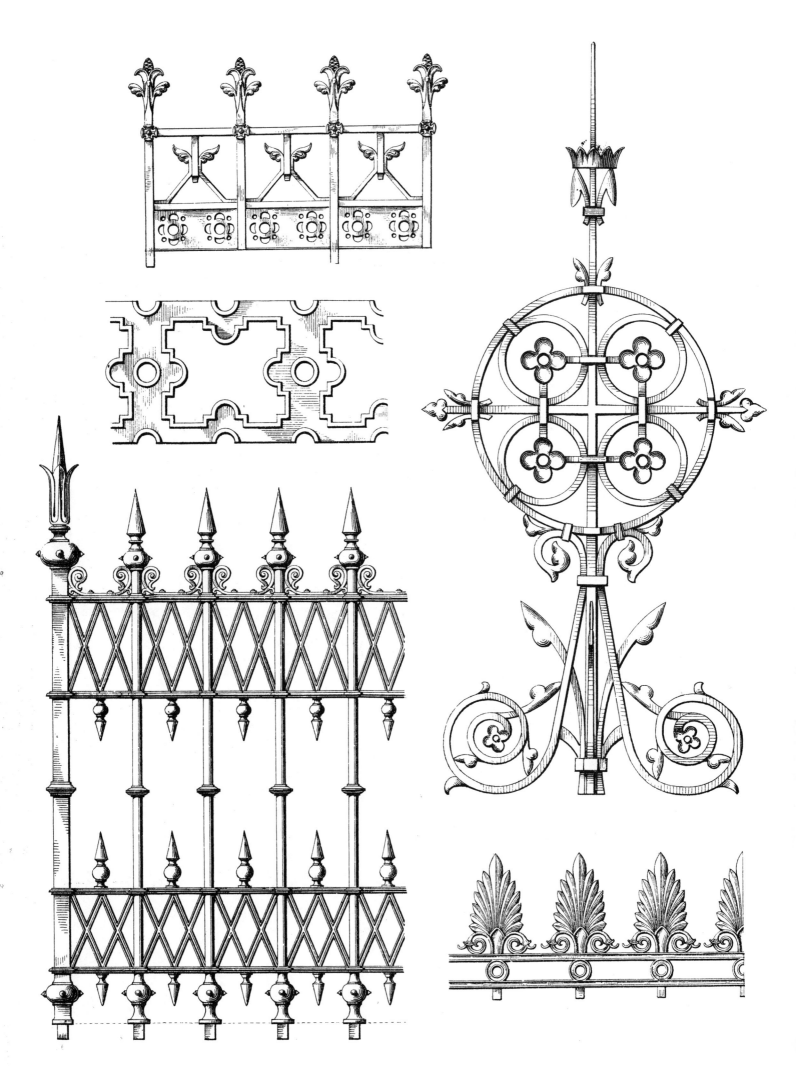

44

45

49

50

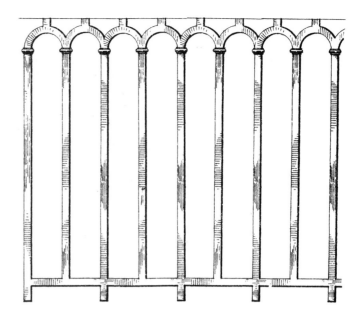

55

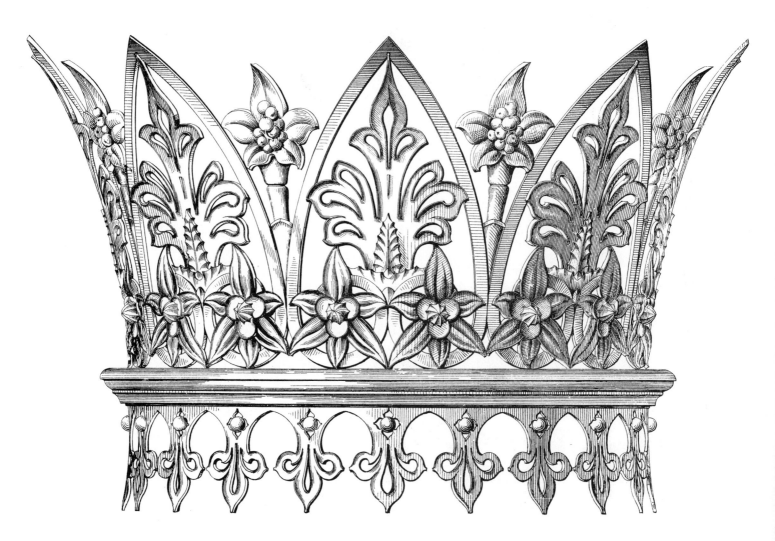

58

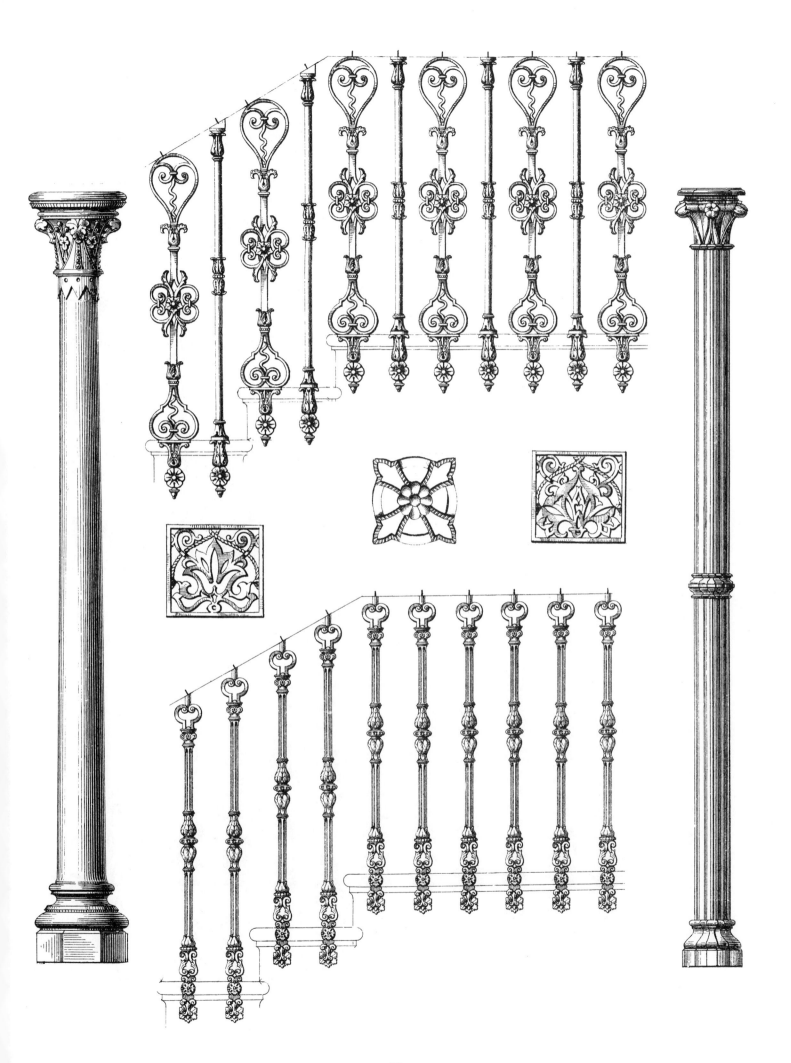

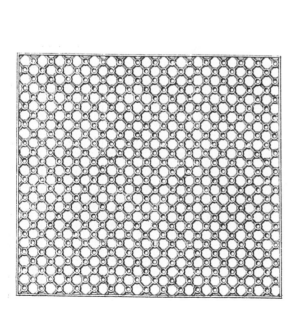

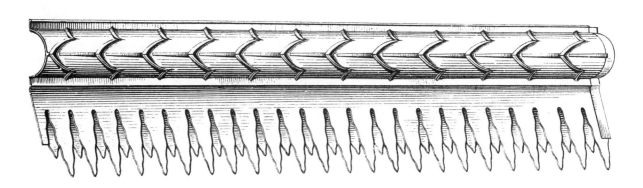

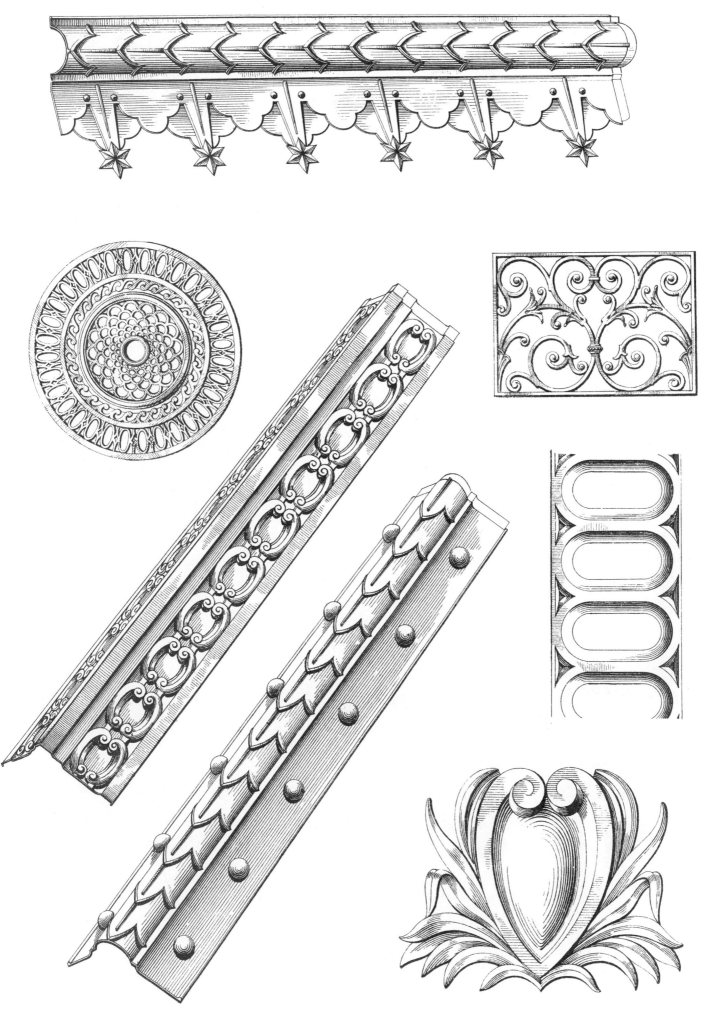

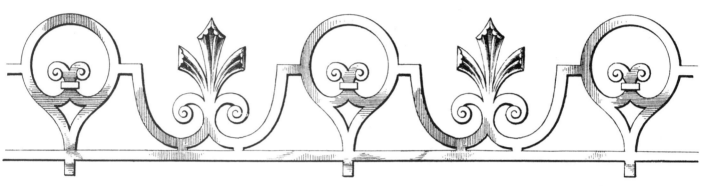

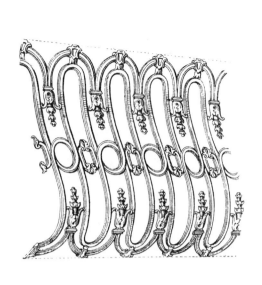

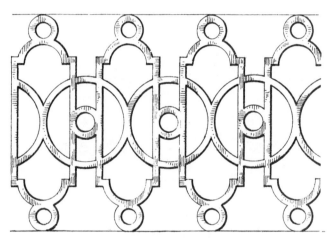

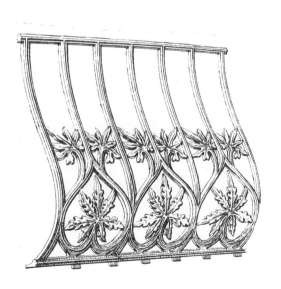

72

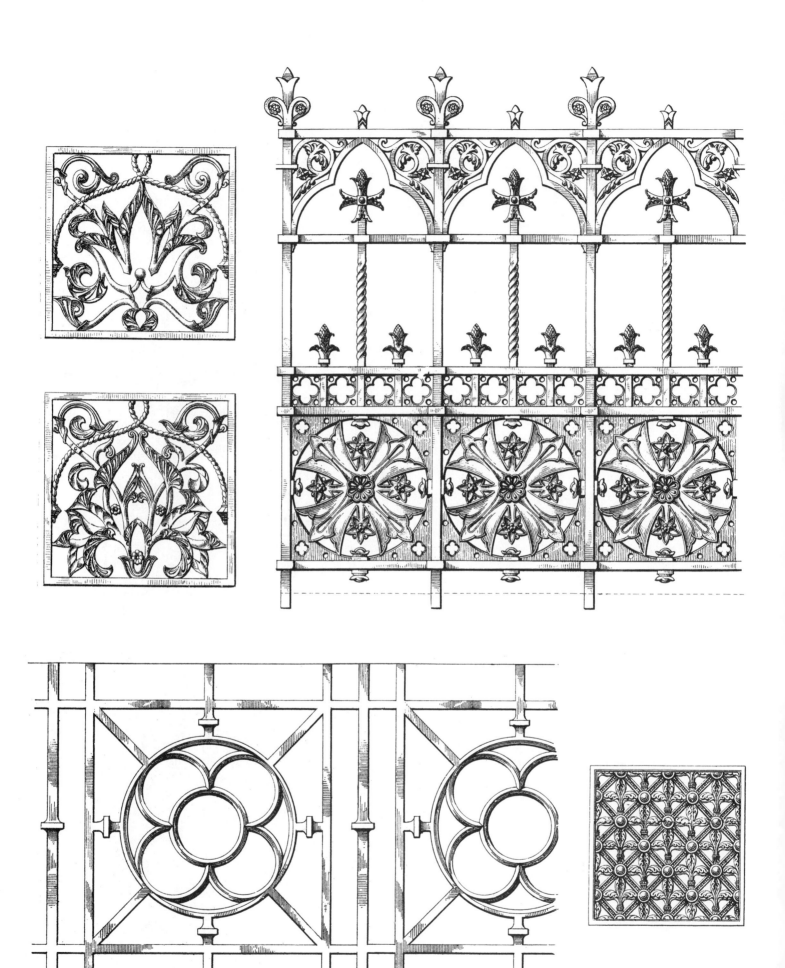

77

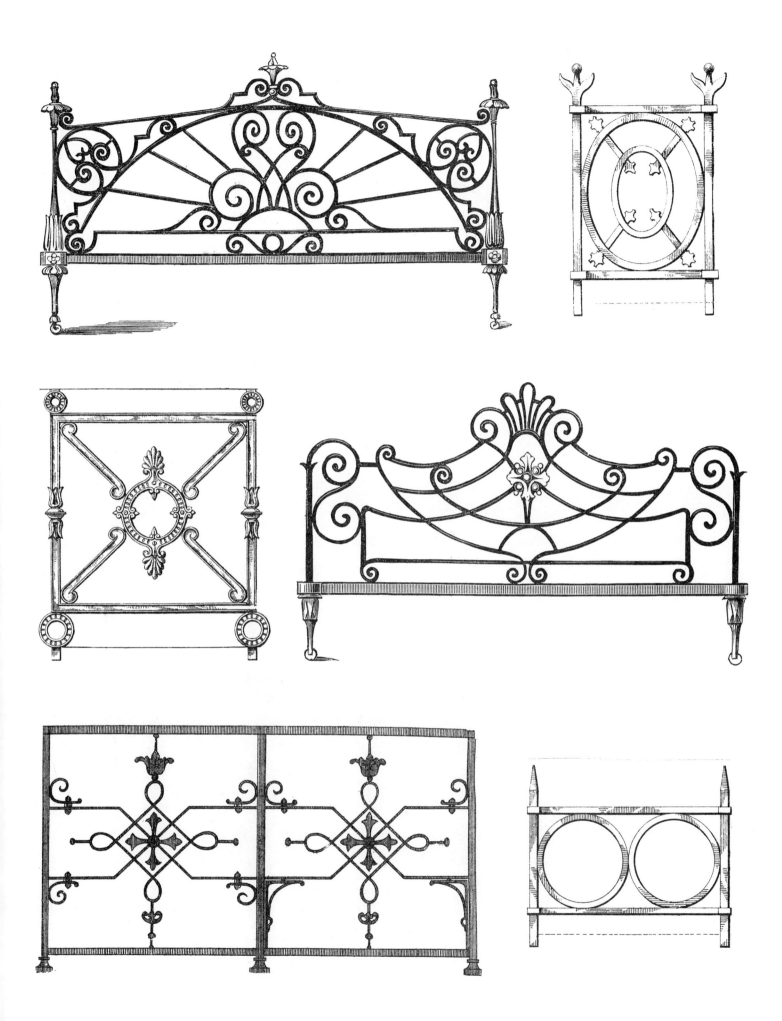

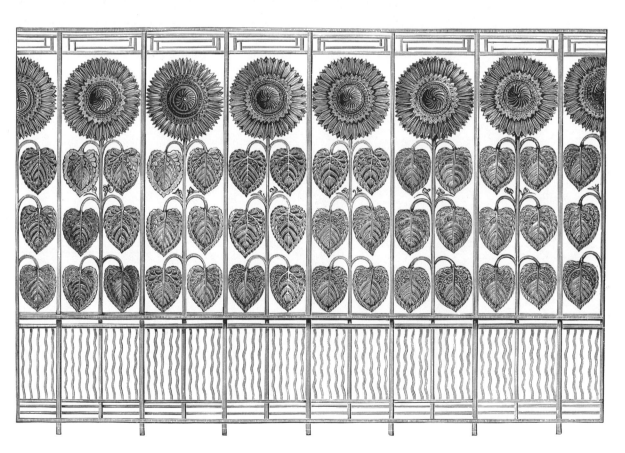

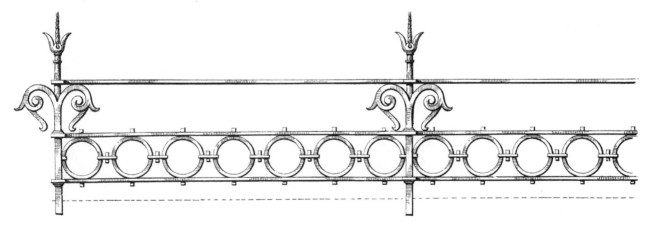

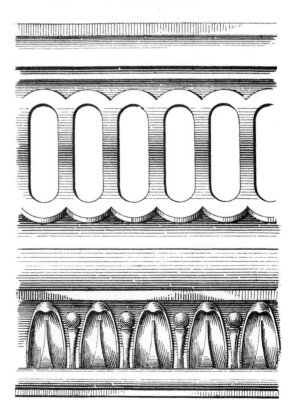

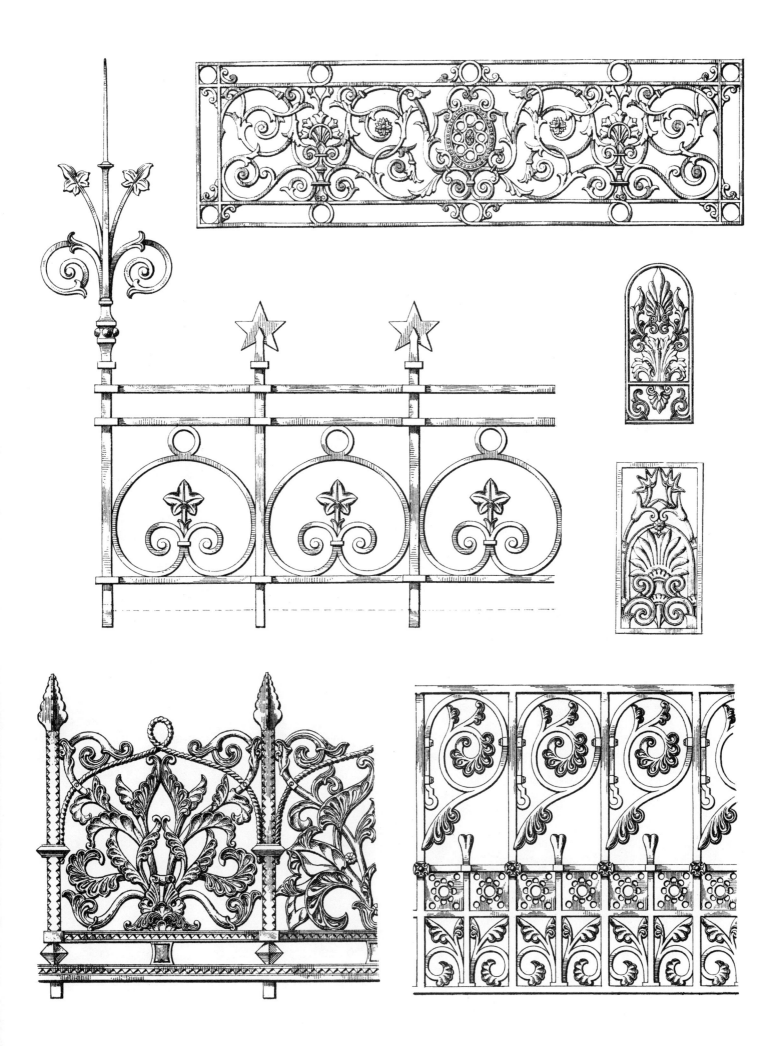

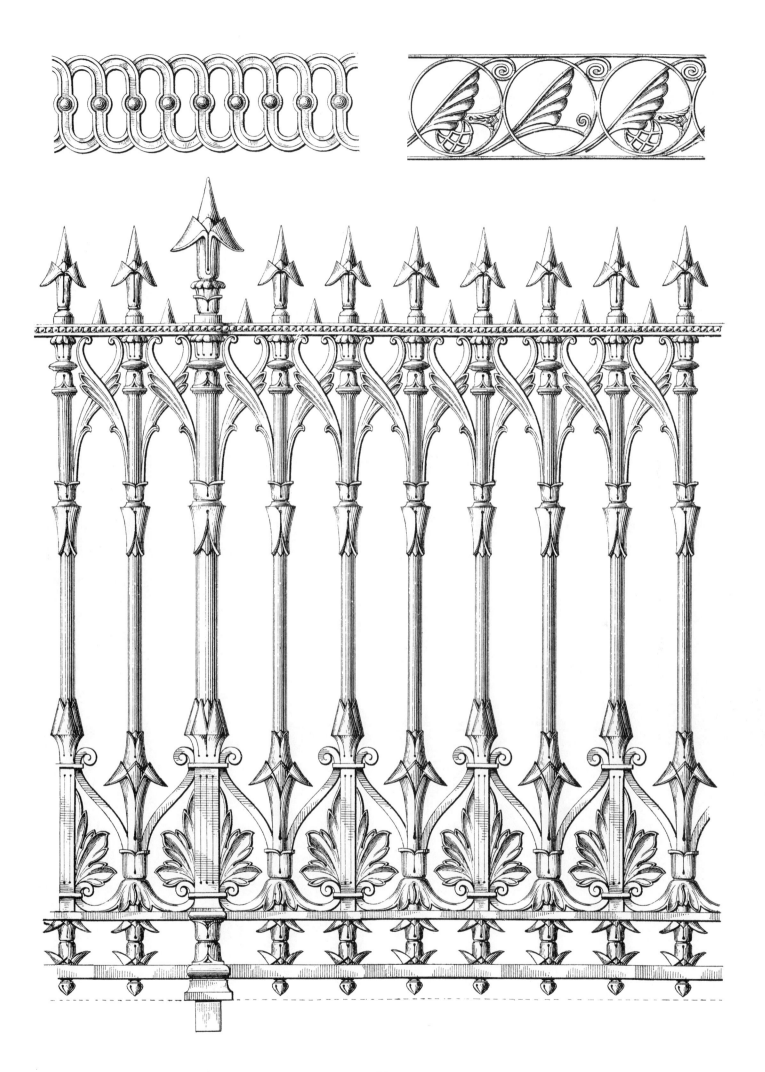

94

95

99

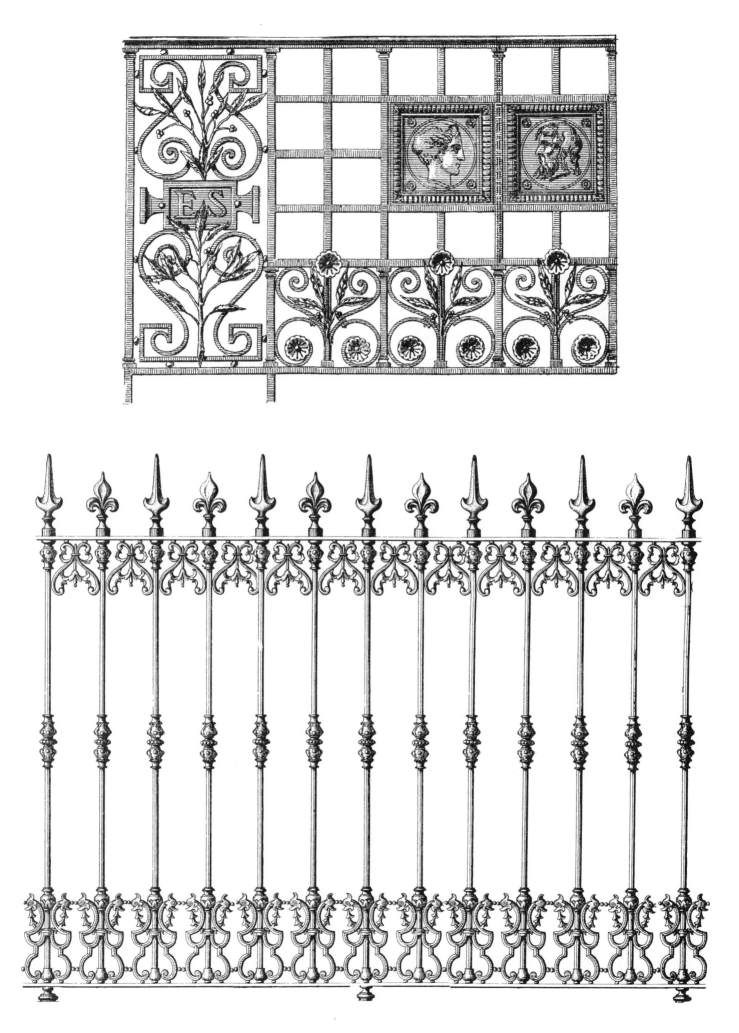

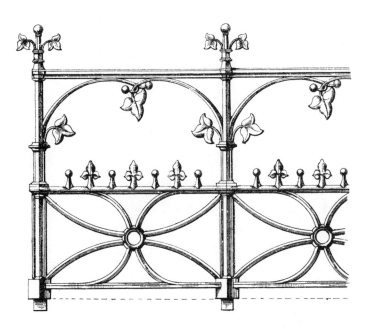

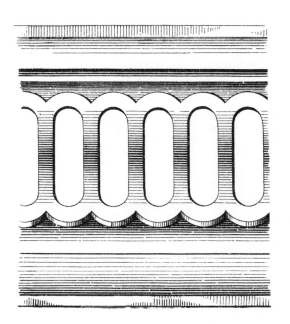

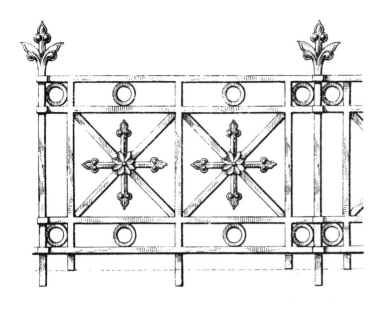

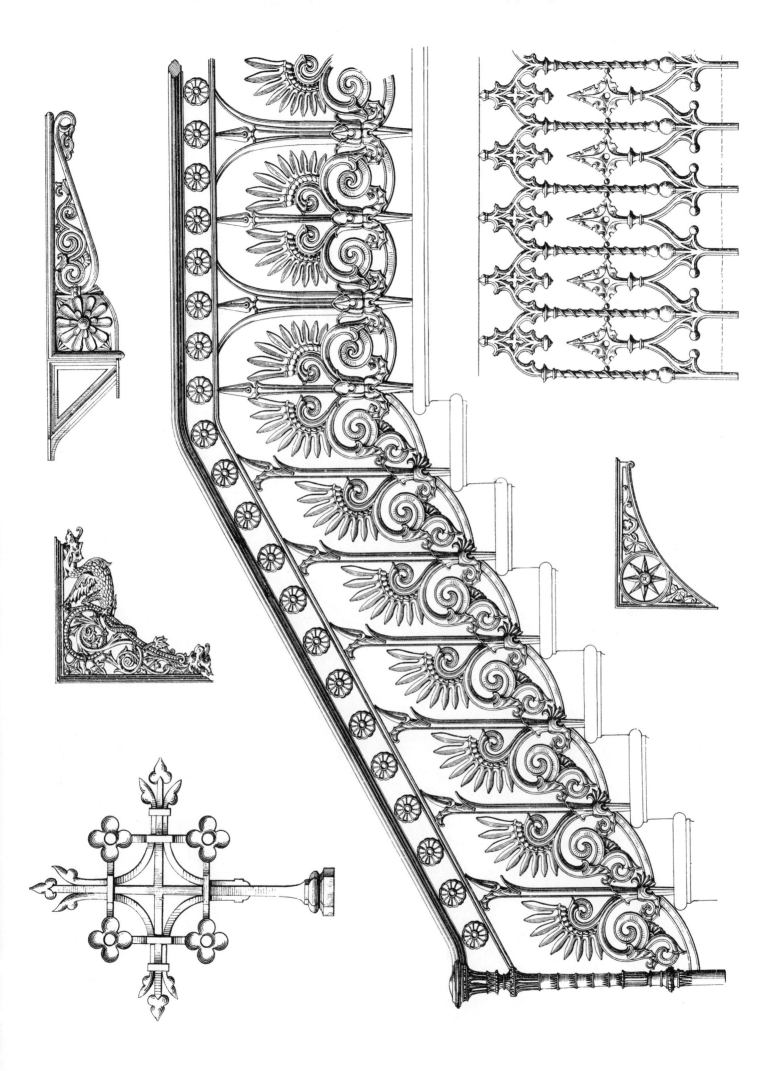

 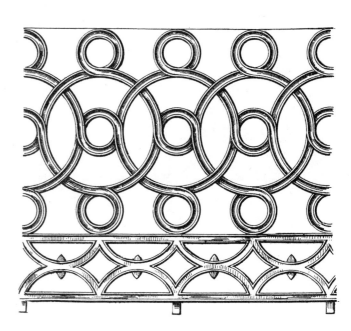

III

116

119

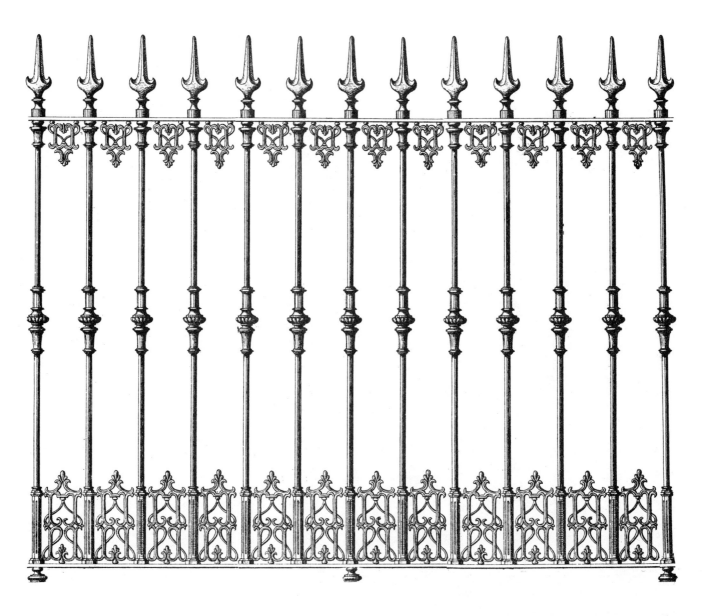

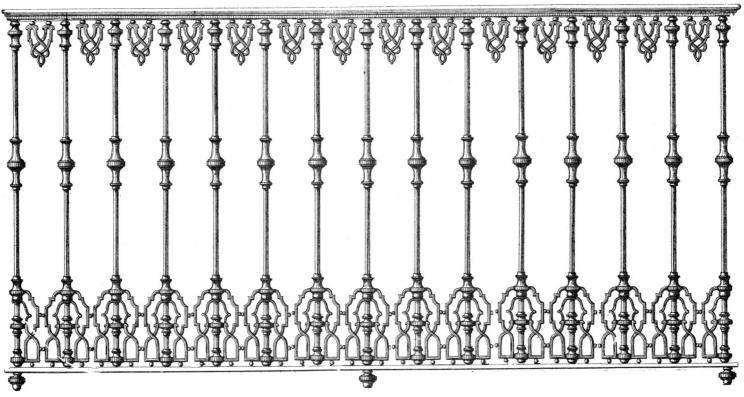